Charlie Brown's Super Book of Things to Do and Collect

Based on the Charles M. Schulz Characters

Random House New York

Designed by Eleanor Ehrhardt
Associates: Terry Flanagan and Charlotte Staub

Copyright © 1975 by United Feature Syndicate, Inc. Produced in association with Charles M. Schulz Creative Associates, Warren Lockhart, President. All rights reserved under International and Pan-American Copyright Conventions. Published in the United States by Random House, Inc., New York, and simultaneously in Canada by Random House of Canada Limited, Toronto. Library of Congress Cataloging in Publication Data. Schulz, Charles M. Charlie Brown's super book of things to do and collect. 1. Collectors and collecting—Juvenile literature. [1. Collectors and collecting. 2. Hobbies] I. Title   AM231.S27   790.13′2   75-7749 ISBN 0-394-83165-9/0-394-93165-3 (lib. bdg.)   Manufactured in the United States of America

Collecting...

Are you a collector?
Almost everyone collects something.
Even three red pencils make a collection!

Collecting is a super hobby.

Here's the Peanuts gang with all kinds of great ideas on how to have fun with a collection — how to start it, what to do with it, and where to keep it.

So hurry up, before everything's gone — join Charlie Brown and start collecting!

Collecting Rocks

How about becoming a rock hound? No, you won't have to move in with Snoopy. A rock hound is just another name for a rock collector.

Collecting rocks is easy because you can find them almost anywhere — in woods and fields, on mountain slopes and beaches, in stream beds, and on deserts. You can even find them in the city — at building sites and road repair sites. You can also buy rock specimens at hobby shops and mineral supply houses.

When Charlie Brown goes rock hunting, he takes along a paper bag to carry back his rocks! Obviously a stronger bag or basket — or even a knapsack — would make a better carrying case. You're sure to find some rocks that are too big and heavy to carry home. In that case, you can easily break off a small piece with a mineral hammer. This tool is sold at hardware stores.

Try to go rock hunting with other rock hounds. It's a lot safer and much more fun. And stick to places that you know well — getting lost is no fun.

At first, you will probably want to collect rocks that have interesting shapes, colors, or textures. But as your collection grows, you may want to organize it better and collect samples of the three basic types of rocks:

1. IGNEOUS   2. SEDIMENTARY   3. METAMORPHIC

When Charlie Brown heard that some igneous rocks come from volcanoes, he refused to have any in his collection. They remind him too much of Lucy. She's been erupting for years! Igneous rocks are formed when magma — a hot, melted material deep in the earth — rises to the surface and cools and hardens. When magma reaches the earth's surface through a crack or volcano, it's called lava. Lava hardens into rocks like basalt and obsidian. Sometimes magma doesn't get quite as far as the surface. Then it cools and hardens underground into such rocks as granite. Since Charlie Brown won't even collect granite, he's missing a sample of one of the hardest rocks of all.

Snoopy, on the other hand, is too sentimental to have sedimentary rocks in his collection. They sometimes contain fossils of plants and animals that lived thousands of years ago. Of course some fossils are more recent than others.

Sedimentary rocks are formed from bits of rock and dead plants and animals that settle on ocean floors and other low-lying places. Gradually this loose material is pressed into rock by the weight of new material that settles on top of it. Sedimentary rock usually forms in layers, called strata. You can often see strata on cliff faces and along highways that cut through hillsides. Limestone and sandstone are two kinds of sedimentary rock.

Some igneous and sedimentary rocks have been changed into a third kind of rock by heat, pressure, and chemicals. This new kind of rock is called metamorphic. Marble is a beautiful metamorphic rock made from limestone. Charlie Brown understands metamorphic rock. He's sure that the pressure from Lucy will make him change some day, too.

7

All rocks are made up of minerals. Usually there's more than one mineral in a rock. Unless they're very finely mixed, you can see the different minerals. Identifying the minerals in a rock helps you to identify the kind of rock. You can find guide books in the library that will help you identify your rocks and minerals.

THE MOHS SCALE

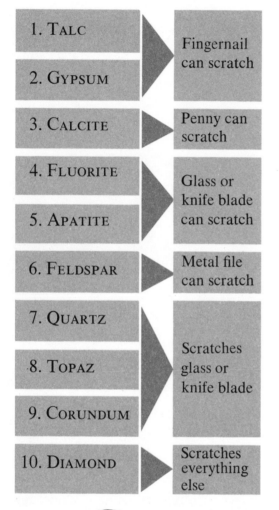

The Mohs Scale	Test
1. TALC	Fingernail can scratch
2. GYPSUM	
3. CALCITE	Penny can scratch
4. FLUORITE	Glass or knife blade can scratch
5. APATITE	
6. FELDSPAR	Metal file can scratch
7. QUARTZ	Scratches glass or knife blade
8. TOPAZ	
9. CORUNDUM	
10. DIAMOND	Scratches everything else

One important clue to a mineral's identification is its hardness. Hardness is ranked according to the Mohs Scale. This scale gives the relative hardness of ten minerals. Talc, which is used in talcum powder, is very soft and is ranked 1. Diamond is the hardest and is ranked 10. One mineral can always scratch another with a lower number. So, to find out the hardness of an unidentified mineral, you try to scratch it with things whose hardness you already know. When you know what can and can't scratch a mineral, you're on your way to identifying it.

Say you have a rock with chunks of a mineral that you think is quartz. Take a copper penny, which ranks 3½ on the Mohs Scale, and try to scratch the mineral. Quartz, which ranks 7, is much harder than a penny. So if you can scratch the mineral with the penny, it isn't quartz — and it certainly isn't a diamond!

When you collect rocks and minerals, you can always be sure of one thing — there are more to be found somewhere . . . even out of this world!

Charlie Brown had one of his few successful ideas when he started a rock collection. He kept all of his rocks in egg cartons. Too bad he didn't stack them up in a safe place!

Schroeder makes his own display cases for his rock collection, and so can you.

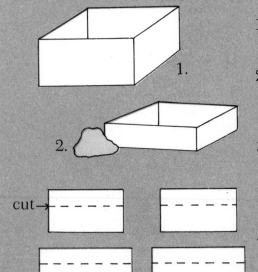

1. Bring home a cardboard carton from a supermarket.

2. Cut the four sides of the box down so they are the same height as the tallest rock you want to display.

3. Take the four strips you just cut from the box and trim them to the same height. Then trim a little off the ends of the strips so they can fit into the box.

4. Cut two notches halfway into each strip. The notches should divide each strip into thirds.

5. Join the four strips crosswise at the notches, and put them in the box.

6. Number the compartments in the box—there will be nine—and put a rock in each compartment.

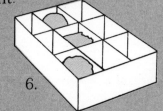

7. Put matching numbers on nine index cards. On each card, name and describe the rock with the same number. Also say when and where you found the rock.

8. You can file your index cards in a shoe box.

You can make things with your rocks, too. Sally makes paperweights.

1. Find a smooth, round, white rock and wash it with soap and water.

2. With a pencil, draw a flower or a bird or any simple design on the rock.

3. Paint the design with tempera paints.

4. After the paint has dried completely, put a coat of shellac over the entire rock. Let the shellac dry overnight before you use the paperweight.

You can also make rock sculptures. Sometimes rock shapes will remind you of something, perhaps a person or an animal. Linus made a turtle out of his rocks. Here's how you can make one:

1. Choose a large, flat rock for the body. Any color will do.

2. Glue on four smaller, flat rocks where feet should be. Use a strong glue.

3. Add a medium-sized rock for the head.

4. After the glue has dried thoroughly, you can paint eyes and a mouth on your turtle's face and markings on its "shell."

5. When the paint is dry, shellac your turtle.

BY LUCY

BY LINUS

All you have to do now is remember that this turtle doesn't like water!

Collecting Dolls and Puppets

Sally had better stick to her dolls. Snoopy just doesn't have the right spirit! Besides, there are all kinds of wonderful dolls and puppets. Some have been around for thousands of years.

Puppets were used in religious ceremonies in ancient Egypt, Greece, and Rome.

Dolls have often been used to display the latest fashions in clothes. About 400 years ago, the French sent fashion dolls to foreign princesses who were to marry French kings. Then the brides knew what kind of clothes to bring to France. Today, life-size dolls called mannequins are used in stores to show the latest styles.

Each country in the world has its own special kinds of dolls and puppets. Every country has some dolls dressed in native costume.

The most famous puppets of all are Punch and Judy. They are two silly, quarrelsome characters who have all kinds of misfortunes. They were first used in puppet shows in England and became popular all over Europe.

The Japanese have puppet shows with *bunraku* puppets that are four feet tall. Usually puppeteers are hidden during a show, but the *bunraku* puppeteers dress in black and stand on a stage in full view of the audience.

11

Very old dolls are hard to find outside of museums. But there are plenty of modern dolls and puppets that you can collect. Buy them or wait for presents— or speed up your collecting by making some! Sally made her own collection of rag dolls and spool dolls and paper puppets and sock puppets. That's Sally for you—she likes to take action!

Here's Sally with one of her rag dolls.
You can make one like it:

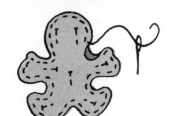

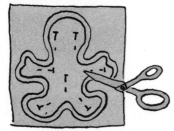

1. Find a large, clean cloth (such as a piece of an old sheet) or buy some new material. A piece 12 inches by 18 inches is a good size, although you can work with any size you like.
2. Fold the cloth in half. If there's a right side to the cloth—a side on which the color or pattern is stronger—make sure it's inside the fold.
3. With a pencil, draw a doll shape on the folded cloth. Then draw a second line around the first, about one-half inch from it.
4. Put some straight pins through the folded cloth, inside the first line you drew. Then cut out the doll shape along the outside line. Cut through both layers of cloth.
5. Sew the two sides of the doll together along the inside line. Use a small running stitch. Leave one shoulder of the doll open.
6. Take out all the straight pins. Then turn the doll inside out through the opening you left in the shoulder.
7. Stuff the doll with scraps of cloth, foam rubber, or absorbent cotton.
8. Poke the edges of the opening back inside. Sew the two sides of the opening together with tiny stitches.
9. Sew colored yarn to the head for hair, and sew on buttons for the eyes, nose, and mouth.

Here's Charlie Brown with his collection of wooden dolls.
He says he made the soldier himself.

You can make all kinds of dolls with wooden clothespins. All you have to do is draw on faces and clothes with felt-tip pens. You can glue things on the dolls, too. Yarn and curled strips of paper make good hair. Toothpicks are good arms. A button makes a hat. A cigar band can be a crown. A piece of shoelace with frayed ends makes a nice scarf. And a vitamin capsule makes an air tank for a deep-sea diver! See what you can think up.

You can also make wooden dolls from empty spools of thread.

1. Glue four spools together end to end to make the body.
2. Cut out two squares of paper for the arms. Roll up each square tightly into a tube and tape the overlapping edge of the paper in place. Tape the arms to the spool body.
3. Glue two spools to the bottom spool to make legs.
4. With felt-tip pens or tempera paints, draw a face on the top spool and a costume on the body.

Peppermint Patty's paper puppets are easy to make, too.
They are finger puppets.

1. Draw an animal or a clown or any figure you like on a piece of heavy paper or light cardboard. Draw circles for ears, arms, or legs—whatever you want your fingers to act as in the puppet.
2. Color the figure and cut it out. Then cut out the circles.

Stick your fingers through the holes and wiggle your puppet's ears,
or walk the puppet away!

Here's a Woodstock favorite—a sock-puppet crocodile.

1. Find an old, green, medium-sized sock. With scissors, cut across the toe and halfway down the sides of the foot, making two flaps for the crocodile's mouth.
2. Holding the sock upside down, sew on two buttons near the heel to make eyes. Sew two small buttons to the end of the upper mouth flap to make a nose.
3. Get a piece of red cloth (felt is best). Fold it in half and pin the two sides together. Then slide the folded edge into the crocodile's mouth as far as you can.
4. Pin the upper mouth flap to the red cloth and trace around it with a pencil or pen.
5. Remove the sock and cut out the shape you just traced. Cut through both layers of cloth, but don't cut open the fold!
6. Slide the folded red shape back into the mouth. Using a hemstitch, sew the upper half of the red shape to the upper mouth flap, and the lower half to the lower mouth flap. Presto! Your crocodile has a red mouth!

Put your hand all the way into the sock.
Your thumb goes under the mouth and your fingers go over it. Now open wide!

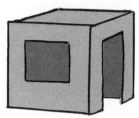

Linus will never give up his blanket, but he doesn't mind using up his old socks! Look at the sock puppet he's made!

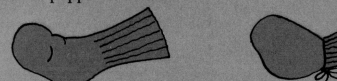

1. Stuff absorbent cotton into the foot of an old sock.
2. Tie thread or string around the sock just beneath the stuffing. Don't tie it too tightly—leave enough room for a finger to reach into the stuffing.
3. Cut eyes, a nose, and a mouth from colored felt. Glue them to the stuffed sock to make a face.
4. Glue yarn to the head to make hair.
5. You can make a hat out of construction paper and glue that to the head, too. (See pages 74-75 for instructions on making hats.)

And now, of course, you need a theater for your puppets, so——

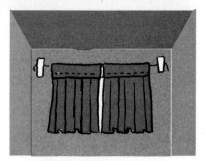

1. Find a very large cardboard carton. An empty washing-machine carton is a good size. Stand it upside down, so that it rests on the open end.
2. Cut a tall rectangle out of one side for a door. Heavy cardboard is hard to cut, so you'll probably have to ask someone to help you.
3. Cut a wide rectangle in the front for the stage opening.
4. To make a curtain, get a piece of cloth that goes two or three inches beyond the stage opening in every direction. Get a piece of string that's several inches longer than the cloth.
5. Cut the cloth in half vertically. Sew or pin the top edge of each piece around the string. Don't sew into the string itself, or you won't be able to open the curtain!
6. Inside the box, tape one end of the string to each side of the stage opening.

Now your curtain is hung and the show can go on!

Collecting Buttons

Button, button, who's got the button?

Buttons are easy to collect. There are so many! You can look for them on old clothes, hunt for them in sewing baskets, get new ones at dime stores or notions stores, and find old ones at antique stores or thrift shops.

Old buttons are interesting to collect because they're often richly decorated, and many have interesting histories. If an old button could talk, imagine what exciting adventures it could tell us! Maybe it was on George Washington's coat when he crossed the Delaware. Maybe it was on the Red Baron's helmet as he attacked from out of the sun.

Lucy has always wondered why buttons are on the left side of her shirts, while Charlie Brown's are on the right side. Well, at one time buttons were all sewed on the left side of garments. During the Middle Ages, however, buttons on men's clothes were changed to the right side. That way a man could quickly unbutton his coat with his left hand and draw his sword with his right. Today clothes are still made the same way—even though no one wears a sword anymore!

Buttons can be made of many different materials—ivory, wood, glass, bone, shell, plastic, leather, or silver, brass, and other metals. In the old days, buttons were often beautifully decorated with mosaics, enamel, precious stones, and even hand-painted portraits.

Look at some buttons. See if you can identify the materials they are made from. Notice the different shapes, colors, and sizes. How are they fastened? Some buttons have metal loops on the back. Others have two or four holes for fastening.

You may want to specialize in your collection, or you may want to collect all kinds of buttons. Here's what Charlie Brown and his friends are collecting.

Sally collects "goofies." These are buttons shaped like figures or objects — such as dogs, cats, horses, or boats.

Schroeder collects old buttons.
Linus collects wooden buttons.
Frieda collects tiny buttons.

Lucy collects buttons with pictures painted on them. She has some with animals, and others with flowers, and still others with portraits of famous people. She is trying to find a button with a portrait of Beethoven to give to Schroeder, but she hasn't had any luck yet.

Snoopy only wants to collect military or uniform buttons. He searches as he prowls the countryside.

Charlie Brown collects any kind of button he can find, whether it is glass, plastic, or shell; whether it is old or new; whether it is large or small. He's not fussy!

Peppermint Patty collects a completely different kind of button. It has words on the front and a pin on the back so she can wear it. You've probably seen people giving this kind of button away on the street before elections, with the name of a candidate printed on the button. Sometimes these buttons have jokes or riddles on them, too.

There are a lot of different ways to display a button collection. Linus makes button cards.

1. Sew the buttons to pieces of colored cardboard, on one side only. You can use either thread or string. Be sure to leave enough space between the buttons so you can write where and when you found each one.

2. File your button cards upright in a cardboard box.

Sally sews her "goofies"
to paper plates.

1. Get paper plates of any size and color you like.

2. Sew some buttons to each plate. You can make the buttons form a picture, or else just sew them into an abstract pattern.

3. Using a hole puncher or a pencil, punch two holes in each plate, one near the top and one near the bottom.

This is a good way to display any kind of button.

4. Tie a loop at one end of a long piece of yarn, and thread the other end through the top of one of the plates. Bring the yarn down behind the plate and out through the bottom hole. Then thread it through the top hole of the next plate, and so on. When all your plates are threaded together, tie a knot at the bottom of the yarn.

5. Use the loop at the top to hang your button plates on a wall.

Lucy divides her buttons according to what is painted on them, and arranges them in clear plastic boxes that she buys. This is a good way to keep your buttons if you think you'll want to trade them with friends.

Charlie Brown has so many buttons, he needs a large container to store them in. So he makes his own — the same way Schroeder makes a display box to hold his rock collection. Turn to page 9 for directions.

If you find a lot of plain buttons of a solid color, try painting your own designs or lettering on them.

1. Using a small paintbrush and tempera paint, paint the design you want on your button.

TEMPERA

VARNISH

2. Let the paint dry completely. Then, with a clean paintbrush, give the button a coat of varnish.

3. When the varnish dries, you can add the button to your collection. Or you can wear it—by sewing it in place or taping a safety pin to the back.

18

Buttons make wonderful jewelry
that you can wear
or give away as gifts.

1. Thread a piece of colored yarn through the holes or loops of your buttons. The yarn should be a long piece if you want a belt or a necklace, and a smaller piece if you want a bracelet.

2. Tie a knot and then a bow with the two ends of the yarn. Wear your handcrafted jewelry!

Schroeder makes his own cuff links.

1. Thread a piece of yarn through a button and knot it.
2. Thread the end of the yarn through another button and knot that.
   You can use any buttons you want to use—it doesn't matter if they match or not.
   Craft stores sell cuff link attachments that can be glued to the back of buttons.

If you can't think of any more things to do with your button collection, you can always sew your buttons onto some of your old clothes. In London, the "button men" cover every inch of their suits and hats with buttons, but you don't have to go that far!

Collecting Flowers

The best thing about collecting flowers is that you can find them everywhere. Wild flowers grow in woods and fields and on beaches and mountains and prairies. They even pop up in the middle of city sidewalks. So start looking!

Try to pick each flower where more of the same kind grow close by. That way, one flower won't be missed. Some flower stems don't break very easily, so cut your flowers with scissors or a penknife.

You can look up each flower's name in a field guide to wild flowers. Use a library book if you don't want to buy your own. Each flower has a scientific name, usually in Latin, and one or more common names. Here are some wild flowers you may find. Maybe you know some of them already.

QUEEN ANNE'S LACE

TRILLIUM

THISTLE

CHICORY

SUNFLOWER

DAISY

Even in winter, when it's hard to find flowers, you can work on your hobby by collecting flower pictures in newspapers and magazines. Learn their names and when spring comes you will recognize the flowers you find for your collection.

If you press your flowers you can keep them in a scrapbook.

Here's how to press them.

1. Place each flower on one side of a few sheets of newspaper or paper towel. Arrange the petals and leaves so that they all face up.

2. Fold the other side of the papers down over the flower.

3. Stack up all your flower "sandwiches" and put some heavy books on top.

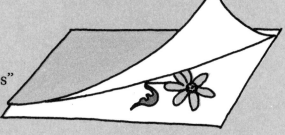

4. After a few days, when the flowers are completely dry, take them out of the papers. Pressed flowers are fragile, so handle them gently.

5. Tape or glue the flowers to the pages of a scrap-book. (If you want to make your own scrapbook, see page 34, instructions 1–4.)

6. Next to each flower write its name (both scientific and common) and where and when you found it.

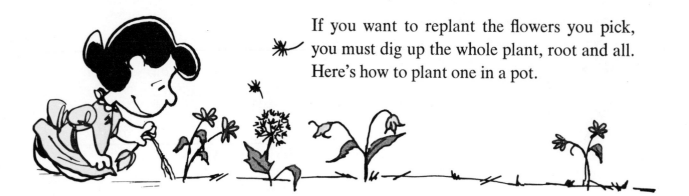

If you want to replant the flowers you pick, you must dig up the whole plant, root and all. Here's how to plant one in a pot.

1. Put a piece of some hard, curved material (such as a piece of a broken clay pot or a sea shell) over the hole in the bottom of a clean flower pot. This will let water drain properly.

2. Hold the flower in the pot so that the top of the root is about half an inch below the rim of the pot.

3. Gently pour soft earth in around the root. (Dig up some garden soil outside or buy potting soil in a dime store or plant store.)

4. Press the soil down gently to make it firm around the plant. Make sure the flower stem is standing up straight.

5. Place the pot on a saucer, and water the flower until some water comes out of the bottom of the pot. Then water again whenever the soil feels dry.

If you found your flower growing in a sunny spot, keep it on a sunny window sill. If it grew in the shade, put the pot on a window sill that gets little or no sun. Wild flowers are usually easy to grow—even if Charlie Brown doesn't think so!

22

If you have extra flowers you can make a potpourri jar. That's a jar filled with fragrant petals from many different kinds of flowers. You can use both wild flowers and garden flowers. Strongly scented flowers are best. A potpourri jar makes a nice present for a special friend—or for someone you'd like to have as a special friend.

1. Pluck the petals from your flowers and let them dry a few days in the open air.
2. Find a small jar with a screw-on cover and fill it with the dried petals. You can also add some whole cloves and bits of dried orange peel.
3. Carefully punch a small hole in the cover of your jar with a hammer and nail.
4. Screw the cover on tight. After a few days there will be a fragrance from all the petals in the jar.

You can make a beautiful collage with pressed flowers. Read how to make collages on page 70. Follow the same instructions but use flowers instead of postcards. Don't forget to add leaves to the collage. You can add other things, too — scraps of cloth, magazine cut-outs, beads — whatever you like.

A bouquet of paper flowers is a nice gift, too. It almost always makes someone happy.

Here's how to make paper flowers.

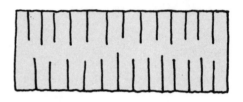

 1 Cut a long, narrow piece of colored tissue paper.

2 Cut slits into both long sides.

3 Gather the tissue paper together the long way.

4 Twist one end of a pipe cleaner around the center. Fan out the "petals."

5 Wind a strip of green construction paper or green tape around the long end of the pipe cleaner to make the stem.

6 Cut leaves out of the green paper.

7 Tape or glue them to the stem.

Try using several pieces of different colored tissue paper together. You can make almost as many kinds of paper flowers as there are real ones!

Flower collecting can be a year-round hobby. Just be sure to keep looking. You never know when a flower will surprise you!

Collecting Bottles

Who ever heard of collecting something that you don't keep? Well, you don't have to keep the bottles you collect! You can take them to a recycling center so the glass can be used again. But some bottles *are* fun to save.

You may want to collect bottles that are very old. Schroeder roams through antique shops and second-hand stores looking for bottles that were used during the American Revolution. Peppermint Patty likes old bottles, too, but she hunts for them at the seashore and in junkyards and vacant lots. That way she not only adds to her collection, but she keeps the bottles from cluttering up the neighborhood.

Some bottles are interesting because of their shape. Linus collects perfume bottles from his friends' mothers. You may want to keep bottles because of the design or lettering on them. Marcie collects bottles from foreign countries. If you have friends or relatives who travel overseas, ask them to bring a bottle back for you.

You can also collect jars, which are really just fat bottles with wide mouths. Some jars have lids with nice designs on them.

Sally collects plastic bottles. Not *all* bottles are made of glass! Charlie Brown's bottle collection is a mixture. He collects any size, shape, or color that strikes his fancy.

One of the nicest ways to display your glass bottles is to line them up on a window sill. Look at the light shining through them. The bottles will cast lovely shadows that change color and shape as the light changes.

You can play music on your glass bottles! Fill some bottles half full with water and line them up according to size. As you hit each one with a spoon, it will make a musical sound. Hitting too hard will produce the sound of breaking glass, so be careful! You can change each bottle's sound by changing the amount of water. Add water to make the tone lower, and pour some water out to make it higher. If you practice, and find just the right water levels, you will be able to play a tune. Try it!

There are all kinds of ways to use and display a bottle collection. Lucy turns some of her bottles into candelholders.

1. Put some glass bottles into a flat-bottomed baking dish.

2. Put a drip candle into the mouth of each bottle. (If you have any old candle stubs, this is a good way to use them up.)

3. Carefully light the candles. Make sure the flames don't touch you or anything nearby.

4. Let the candles burn down completely. The melted wax will drip down the sides of the bottles.

5. Put new candles of different colors in the mouths of the bottles. If any small stubs remain from the old candles, pry them out first—or just stick the new candles on to them.

6. Keep burning candles until your bottles are covered with a rainbow of wax.

Now your decorated bottles are ready to be used as candleholders. Put new candles of any kind in them. Light the candles on special occasions.

Sally made a piggy bank from an empty plastic bleach bottle.

1. Turn a plastic bottle on its side. Carefully cut two slits near the mouth of the bottle.

2. Cut small triangles from cardboard to make ears. Slide a triangle into each slit.

3. Twist a pipe cleaner around your finger to make a curly tail.

4. Punch a small hole at the other end of the bottle, opposite the ears. Put one end of the pipe cleaner into the hole.

5. Cut a three-inch slit in the middle of the bottle between the ears and the tail.

6. Glue four corks to the bottom of the bottle to make feet.

7. Put a big cork in the mouth of the bottle to make a snout.

8. Paint your bottle with tempera paints.

What do you think Sally does with the money she saves in her bottle piggy bank? She buys more bottles!

Charlie Brown put a message into a bottle at the beach last summer, and he's still waiting for a reply. If you do this, put your name and address on the message. Charlie Brown forgot to do that!

Collecting Bottle Caps

If you're collecting bottles you may want a bottle caps collection, too. Peppermint Patty likes the way they look in a glass jar, and Sally thinks they sound good in a paper bag. Soda pop caps are fun, but you can also collect caps from other kinds of bottles and even from jars. Charlie Brown was so anxious to start a collection that he forgot to eat the last pickle and use the last drop of ketchup before he took the caps!

A soft drink stand is a good place to collect bottle caps with a particular brand name. In just one day (a very hot one) Peppermint Patty collected 678 caps — 421 of them were the same kind! You can collect very old bottle caps, which is what Linus does. He finds them in junk shops. Or you can specialize in bottle caps from foreign countries, as Lucy does. If your friends can't carry a bottle back from their travels, ask them to bring a few bottle caps for you.

A bottle cap collage is a good way to display part of your collection.

1. Flatten out some of your bottle caps with a hammer. Be careful!
2. Arrange the flat ones, and some that you haven't flattened, on a piece of heavy cardboard. You can show the inside of some of your caps, too.
3. Glue the caps to the cardboard with strong white glue or rubber cement.
4. Let the glue dry completely. Then tape a piece of twine to the back of the cardboard so you can hang your collage on the wall.

Like any collage, a bottle cap collage can have all kinds of other things on it, too. You can see what one collage looks like on page 70.

You can make musical instruments with your collection.
Schroeder makes tambourines.

1.-2.

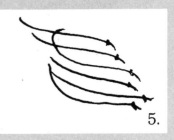

5.

1. With a pencil, punch six holes around the edge of a paper plate.
2. Paint a design on the plate with tempera paints. Let the paint dry completely.
3. Flatten six of your bottle caps with a hammer. Be careful!
4. Punch a hole through the middle of each flattened cap with a hammer and nail. Then take twelve unflattened caps and punch holes in them, too.
5. Cut six short pieces of heavy string. Tie a knot in one end of each string.
6. Put three caps on each piece of string. A flat cap should go in the middle, with an unflattened cap on each side of it.
7. Thread each string of caps through a hole in the paper plate and tie a knot to keep it in place.
Make music!

3.

4.

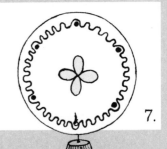

6.

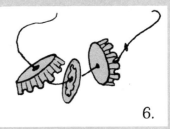

7.

Sally makes musical jewelry with her collection.

1. Very carefully punch a hole through some clean bottle caps with a hammer and nail.

2. Thread the caps onto a piece of colored yarn. The yarn should be long enough for a bracelet, or a necklace, or a belt, depending on what you want to make.

3. Tie the ends of the yarn in a knot and then a bow.

Trade your extra bottle caps with friends who have collections of their own.
Peppermint Patty is the bottle cap champ!
If you're a champ, see page 18 to make your own champ button.

Collecting Stamps

"Neither snow, nor rain, nor heat, nor gloom of night stays these couriers from the swift completion of their appointed rounds." Right! The mail always gets through, but not without a postage stamp.

Stamp collecting is an easy hobby to start. Just ask for all the stamps on the mail your family receives. Ask your friends and relatives to save stamps for you, too. You can also ask business people in your town if they will give you the stamps on their letters. Some of the mail may be from foreign countries and that means foreign stamps for your collection. If you prefer, you can start your collection by buying stamps at a hobby store or dime store. You can always buy current United States stamps at the post office, of course. After you've collected for a while, you may want to start buying special stamps from a stamp dealer.

The first postage stamp was issued by Great Britain in 1840 and stamp collecting probably started then, too.

Legend says that the first stamp collector was a British girl who wanted to wallpaper her bedroom with stamps. Lucy must have heard about her!

Since 1840 millions of different postage stamps have been issued. Different countries have their own traditions with stamps. For example, in the United States no living person is ever shown on a stamp, but famous people in our history are honored by placing their portraits on stamps. Great Britain is the only country that doesn't put its name on its stamps. Instead, the current king or queen appears on all of them. Some stamps have famous places on them. Others celebrate historic moments or special events. These are called "commemorative" stamps. Almost anything you are interested in can be found on a stamp.

Stamps are very fragile, so they must always be handled carefully. Never try to pull a stamp off an envelope, as you may damage it. Just soak the envelope in cold water for fifteen minutes and the stamp will come off easily.

You can avoid getting your stamps dirty or creased by handling them with stamp tongs. Store your loose stamps in envelopes, where they'll stay flat and clean.

You may want to specialize in your collection. Naturally, Peppermint Patty collects stamps with animals on them.

Sally's the nature lover in the group. She collects floral stamps, and also stamps showing rocks and minerals.

Charlie Brown managed to find some stamps with sports pictures on them.

You can imagine what's on Snoopy's stamps!

Linus specializes in stamps illustrated with famous works of art.

Look who Schroeder found on a stamp!

Stamp collectors—or philatelists, as they are called—refer to stamps as "unused" or "used." An unused stamp has not been used as postage.

A used stamp has been used as postage and therefore has a cancellation mark on it. Unused stamps are usually more valuable.

Stamps vary in value depending on how many of each kind are available and what their condition is. The most valuable stamp in the world was issued in 1856 by British Guiana. There is only one copy of it, and it is now worth $280,000. Look at your stamps carefully. Occasionally there is a printing error. In 1918, the pictures on a sheet of United States air mail stamps were printed upside down, and in 1971 just one stamp from that sheet sold for $36,000! If Charlie Brown had one of these, he'd probably use it on a letter as postage!

If you look at a stamp under a magnifying glass, you will be surprised to see how detailed it is.

There are so many other interesting things to learn about stamps that you'll find it helpful to read a library book about stamp collecting. (Some good stamp guides are listed in the back of this book.) In the library you can also find a stamp catalog. Use this to identify your stamps.

The best place to keep your stamps is in an album. You can buy one made especially for stamps in any hobby shop.

You can also make your own stamp album, as Charlie Brown did.

1. Use sheets of colored construction paper for the pages in the album —as many as you want. Use two more sheets (or two pieces of colored cardboard) for the front and back covers.
2. With a hole puncher or a pencil, punch two holes in one long side of each sheet of paper. Make sure the holes are in the same place on every sheet!
3. Line up all the pages inside the covers. Thread a piece of colored yarn through each set of holes, and tie the loose ends in a bow.

4. Write the title of the album on the cover.

5. Decide which stamps you want on each page. Group them by subject or by country.

6. Attach your stamps to the pages with hinges. (You can buy stamp hinges at a hobby store or dime store.) Moisten the short end of the hinge and stick it to the back of the stamp, at top.

7. Then moisten the hinge's long end and press it onto the album page. If you ever want to remove a stamp from your album, just peel the hinge from the page.

As you learn which of your stamps are easier to replace than others, and which are more valuable, you may decide not to keep some. Don't throw them away! You can trade them with other stamp collectors.

There are other things you can do with stamps, too. Maybe you'd like to try Franklin's idea. He hung up a large map of the world and pasted his extra stamps on the countries they came from.

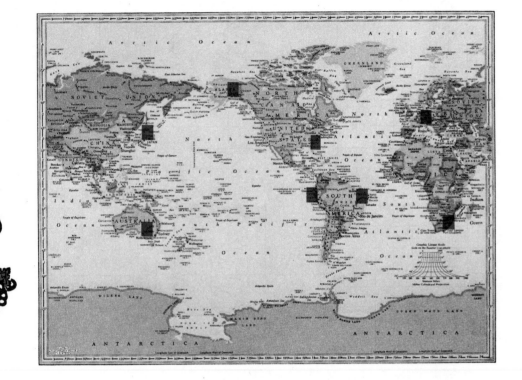

Linus likes to decorate household objects with stamps. He covers trays and jars with them.

1. Glue stamps to the object you want to cover. Use rubber cement if the stamps no longer have gum on them. The stamps can overlap each other or they can be cut to fit.

2. Let the glue dry completely. Then give the object a coat of shellac with an old paint brush.

You can even use a stamp-covered box to store your extra stamps!

Every year more and more stamps are issued, so your collection can get bigger and bigger and bigger!

Collecting Shells

Some of the most unusual homes in the world are the beautiful shells that house the animals of the sea.

The mysterious way that shells are created makes them fascinating. And so does their variety. There are more than 100,000 different kinds of shells!

You can hunt for shells along the shores of oceans, lakes, or rivers. The best time to go shelling at the ocean is at low tide, especially after a storm when the waves have tossed shells onto the beach. Your pockets probably won't be big enough to carry all the shells you'll find, so bring along a plastic bag or a basket. Sometimes shells are hidden in seaweed or under rocks. Sometimes they are buried in sand or mud, and you have to dig for them. Often they are right under your feet—so watch where you walk. Charlie Brown would have had a beautiful clam shell, but he stepped on it!

A shell is a protective case formed by animals called mollusks. Some mollusks, like clams, have two matching shells which they can open. So don't be surprised if you pick up a double shell and it snaps shut! As you walk along the beach, you may see little spurts of water coming up from the damp sand. This means a double-shelled mollusk is burrowing down below.

The shells that still have live animals in them are usually in the best condition. But when you begin your collection, gather all the shells you find. You can always replace an imperfect shell when you find a better one.

Different shells are found in different parts of the United States and the world. Remember to tell your friends and relatives that you are collecting shells, and ask them to bring back some choice specimens from their travels. Of course, you can always trade shells with friends who have the same hobby. Some collectors buy shells that they can't find in their area.

The color, shape, and size of a shell will help you identify it. There are so many different shells that you will need a guide book to see what yours are called. You can borrow a field guide from the library or buy one. The common name of a shell may vary from place to place, so most collectors identify their shells by their scientific names.

Some shells are so small that they can fit comfortably on the head of a pin. A few, like the Florida Horse Conch, grow as long as two feet. And the giant clam of the South Pacific Ocean can grow four feet long!

Look closely at your shells—each one is a very special creation. Sally's collection is quite impressive—particularly to Charlie Brown, who's only found one broken clam shell.

All shells should be cleaned. If there are no animals in your shells, all you have to do is wash them with soap and water. Shells with animals still inside them need very careful cleaning.

1. Put the shells in a pan of warm water. Bring it to a boil, and boil for five minutes. Then let the water cool.

2. Pick out the animals with a bent hairpin or safety pin. Be careful not to damage the shells.

3. Soak the shells in a solution of household bleach (one cup of liquid bleach to two quarts of water) to remove the smell. Be careful not to get bleach in your eyes or on your skin.

4. Rinse the shells in cool water, and let them dry.

Now you'll want to show off your collection. Here's how to make a display case like Sally's.

1. Remove the lids from some matchboxes and glue the boxes together, side by side.

2. Glue the bottoms of the matchboxes to a piece of cardboard.

3. Cut pieces of white paper to fit in the boxes.

4. Choose the shells that you want to display. Write the name of each shell, and when and where you found it, on a white paper, and set the shell on it in a box.

For your larger shells you can make display cases from cartons, just as Schroeder did for his rock collection. See page 9.

North American Indians made wampum beads from clam shells and used them for decoration and money. Peppermint Patty strings shells together and makes jewelry for the gang. Here's how you can make some:

1. Thread a large needle with a piece of colored yarn. The length of the yarn depends on whether you want to make a necklace, a bracelet, or a belt.

2. Tie a knot at one end of the yarn.

3. Carefully push the needle through the center of some of your very thin shells.

4. Unthread the needle and tie the two ends of the yarn into a bow.

Franklin gathers every shell he can find and puts the broken ones into glass jars. You can put shells of the same color into a jar, or mix colors and sizes. Place the jars around your room. Jars of thin shells look lovely on window sills when the light shines through them.

Marcie makes shell animals.

1. Pick out some shells that remind you of parts of an animal.

2. Glue them together to make a little animal statue.

3. Let the glue dry completely. Then you can paint features on the shell face with tempera paint.

Lucy makes mosaics with some of her small shells.

1. With a pencil, draw a picture or design on a small piece of heavy cardboard.

2. One by one, glue tiny, colorful shells onto the board, filling in the spaces of your picture. You can use whole shells and broken shells. Don't leave any pencil marks showing.

3. You can also glue shells all over the background of the picture. Pick colors that will let the picture stand out against the background.

41

Collecting Maps

A map is a picture that shows where things are.

Maps are great to collect because there are so many kinds.

There are road maps that show travelers which roads to take to get from one town to another. If you stick close to home like Snoopy you won't need one, but a map is very helpful to world travelers like Charlie Brown. If you know how to read a map you won't ever get lost.

Some maps show the routes that railroads and buses take.

Airplane pilots use maps to direct their course from city to city.

Sailors use maps called nautical charts to steer their ships into harbors.

Builders use maps called blueprints to build houses and plan towns.

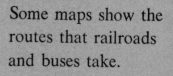

Some maps show places of historical interest.

The weather is recorded and predicted on maps. Weather maps have symbols for rain, snow, clouds, sun, and wind direction.

On all maps any measurements, directions, and symbols are explained in the "key."

Almost every map has a scale of measurement on it. This tells you how the size of the map relates to the actual size of whatever the map shows. The scale is often printed as a straight line with units marked off on it. If you see a scale printed 0 10 20, then you know that a distance ⊢——⊣ long on the map represents ten miles.

Many maps have a compass printed on them. It usually looks like this:

N   stands for North
S   stands for South
E   stands for East
W   stands for West

Here are some symbols you may see on maps:

CAMPSITE
STATE CAPITAL
ROADSIDE PARKS
AIRPORT

There are a lot of ways to collect maps. Lucy visits gas stations on her roller skates looking for road maps.

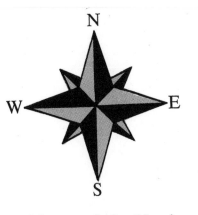

You can, too, though you'll probably find it easier to ride your bike! Most gas stations give out free road maps. You can also buy maps at bookstores, card shops, and newspaper stands. Some cities even have special map stores.

Almost every town in the United States has a Chamber of Commerce. Write to as many as you wish for their local maps. This is a wonderful way to learn about your country.

You can also write to state highway departments, automobile clubs, tourist information offices, travel organizations, airlines, and oil companies. The U.S. Geological Survey and the U.S. Weather Bureau in Washington, D.C., are good sources of low-cost maps.

Ask all your friends to bring maps for you from their travels. Of course, you be sure to collect maps when you go on a trip. After you're back home, you'll always be able to recall your trip just by looking at your maps. If you take that trip again, you can be the navigator and plan the best route to take.

Once you have a lot of maps, you'll need a place to keep your collection.

1. Find a good-sized cardboard box, such as a large envelope box or a boot box.
2. Put your folded maps in the box, on end. Group them by subject or area, or file them alphabetically.
3. Make out an index card for each map. It can read:

MAP OF_____

I GOT THIS MAP FROM_____

ON_____

4. Number your maps and your index cards so that they match each other.
5. Keep the index cards in a shoe box. Now you can quickly check which maps you have and where they are in the map file.

You can also store your maps open. Some maps are too interesting to keep folded up, so here is a way to keep them open and still neat. Linus keeps his this way.

1. Get two pieces of heavy paper. Each should be big enough to cover your largest map.

2. Put one piece of paper exactly on top of the other, and tape the two together along one edge.

3. Put your open maps inside your new folder, and slide it under your bed for safekeeping.

Try making your own maps!

The easiest map to begin with is one of a route you know well. Make a map that shows the route you take from your home to your school.

1. Draw an X on one corner of a piece of paper. This X marks your starting point, at home.

2. Draw lines to show the street where you live.

3. Write in the name of the street. Draw an arrow on the street to show the direction in which you walk to school.

4. Every time you turn a corner, draw the next street you walk on. Add its name and an arrow to show your new direction.

5. Draw squares for buildings that you know along the way. Finish with a square for your school.

6. How accurate is your map? Follow it home after school by walking the opposite way your arrows point.

Peppermint Patty had to draw her map three times before it was right. So don't be disappointed if your map leads you to the wrong house!

You can also make a "relief" map—a three-dimensional map—using soap flakes. Sally and Linus made a huge one! But it's best to start small. Your map can be of a place you know or of an imaginary world.

1. Find a shallow cardboard box or box lid.

2. Lay out some newspapers where you're going to work.

3. In a bowl, mix 2 cups of soap flakes with ¾ cup of water until you have a smooth paste.

4. Cover the bottom of your box with the soap paste. It should be about ¼ inch deep. If you haven't got enough paste, mix up another batch.

5. Build your map on the soap base. Use more soap paste to make mountains or buildings. With your finger or a spoon handle, draw rivers or streets in the soap. You can make surfaces smooth by dipping your fingers in water and rubbing them on the soap.

6. Let your map dry overnight. Then, if you like, you can paint it with thick tempera paint.

7. You can also decorate your map with little figures, trees, fences, street signs—whatever you like. You can use toothpicks to build a lot of things. For example, glue some paper shapes to toothpicks to make street signs. Bits of green sponge glued to toothpicks make good trees. Then just stick the toothpicks into place in the soap.

TREASURE HUNT TODAY

Now that you know how to make maps, you can hold a treasure hunt. Hide a treasure somewhere in your house or neighborhood. Then make a map showing how to find it, and give copies to all your friends. You can use anything you want for the treasure. Lucy used Linus' blanket. If the treasure had been a candy bar, Snoopy might have tried harder to find it!

Collecting Place Mats and Menus

What's the next best thing to eating when you go out for dinner? Right! Adding another menu or place mat to your collection.

There are all kinds of fascinating place mats and menus. Restaurants have them, of course, but so do airplanes and cruise ships. Sometimes menus and place mats are designed for special occasions — private parties, banquets, state dinners at the White House. You'll find some that have riddles, puzzles, and games on them. Others show scenes or famous paintings. Some have maps on them, or historical facts. And some are just decorative.

Menus and place mats can be very simple or very fancy. Some menus have even won awards for being so well designed.

If you're lucky, you can find old menus in secondhand bookstores. Or maybe you can convince someone to give you an old one — people often save menus as souvenirs of their trips. It's interesting to compare the way menus are written today with the way old ones were written. Compare the prices, too—that's *really* interesting!

48

When you eat out, ask your waiter for a souvenir place mat or menu. Most restaurants are happy to give these to customers. You can also write to hotels in the United States and all over the world. Just say you are a collector and ask if they will send you a place mat and menu. Then you will see what people in other states and countries like to eat. Of course, you'll probably have to learn a little French, Italian, German, or Japanese so you can understand a foreign menu!

The whole Peanuts gang has gone to the International Restaurant. The waiters there speak eight foreign languages!

Lucy is starting her meal off with a French soup. Linus wants to try a Danish specialty for his appetizer. Franklin has ordered a vegetable in Italian. Peppermint Patty has asked for her favorite Hungarian dish. Schroeder has ordered his main course in Beethoven's language — German. Charlie Brown has asked in Spanish for a little something on the side. Sally is showing off by ordering a Greek dessert. Not to be outdone, Snoopy has written the Japanese word for his dessert on his napkin. You can find out what they all ordered on page 80.

You'll need a place to keep your collection. Why not make a special scrapbook for it? You'll find instructions for making one on page 72. A favorite menu or place mat also looks great as a wall decoration, so hang up part of your collection!

Don't forget to ask your family and friends to save menus and place mats for you. Here's someone who never misses the chance to get a menu…or a meal!

Collecting Coins

Lucy collects nickels . . . most of them from Charlie Brown!

You can collect nickels, too—or dimes or pennies. You can also collect coins from other countries. They are sometimes very different from United States coins in size or shape or design. Ask any world travelers you know to bring a coin home for you.

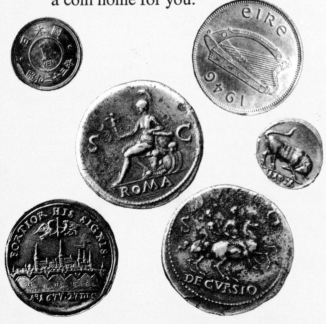

Coin collecting began hundreds of years ago when foreign coins were part of the booty brought home by victorious armies. People were fascinated by them and started to save them, and coin collecting got its start.

Coins are a record of the history of our country and of the world. Before the American Revolution, England wouldn't supply coins to the American Colonies and didn't want them to make their own, so all kinds of foreign coins were used. Among them was the Spanish silver dollar.

It was called a "piece of eight" because it was often cut into pieces, or bits, to make change. There were eight bits in one dollar. Therefore, a half of a dollar was a four-bit piece and a quarter of a dollar was a two-bit piece. That's why even today a United States quarter is still called "two bits."

In 1793 the first coins with the imprint "United States of America" were made in Philadelphia. They were designed with the figure of Liberty on the front and a wreath on the back.

A portrait of George Washington had been considered for the front, but he didn't want himself or any other living person to be pictured. That is why, to this day, there are no portraits of living people on any United States coins. Lucy is furious about that. She may never forgive George Washington. She thinks her face would be perfect on a silver dollar.

"Proof" coins are made especially for collectors. They have a mirrorlike finish and are never supposed to be used.

There are "commemorative" coins which are made to celebrate historic events. They can't be used as money.

51

Coin collectors are called numismatists. Here are a few of the special terms they use when they talk about coins.

OBVERSE

INSCRIPTION
FIELD

REVERSE

REEDED EDGE

FIELD—The field is the background.
INSCRIPTION—The inscription is all the writing.
OBVERSE—Obverse is the front (or heads) side.
REVERSE—Reverse is the back (or tails) side.
REEDED EDGE—The reeded edge means the ridges on the edge.

You may want to start by collecting pennies —or cents, as numismatists call them.

One of the things to look for on a penny is the "mint mark." This mark tells where a United States coin was minted, or made. The mint mark is a small capital letter. On a penny, it appears underneath the date. A small D means the coin was minted in Denver. A small S means it was minted in San Francisco. If you don't find any mint mark, you know it was made in Philadelphia—a mark isn't put on pennies minted there.

Another thing to look for is the initials of the artist who designed the Lincoln cent, Victor D. Brenner. You can find them on some of the Lincoln cents that have ears of wheat on the reverse. Usually they're directly under Lincoln's shoulder. Woodstock can never find them.

You can find coins for your collection by looking through your change every time you buy something. Ask your family to empty their pockets at night and show you their small change. You can get rolls of coins at banks if you want to search through a lot quickly. If you need a few special coins to complete a set, you can buy them from coin dealers.

Coins that are well taken care of are worth more to a collector. Try to handle your coins by the edges so they don't get dull or scratched. Never polish a coin, as that can scratch it. If you want to clean a coin, just wash it with plain soap and water.

Keep each of your coins in a separate container so they don't rub against each other. You can buy cardboard folders or small boxes at a hobby shop, but envelopes are just as good.

You will find coin guide books in your library. They'll tell you what to look for on each coin, how each came to be designed and minted, and how valuable each is.

There are many coins that are worth more than the value printed on them. A coin's value depends on how old it is, how many others there are like it, and what condition it is in. That can be anywhere from Extremely Fine to Fair.

It is difficult to find very valuable coins, but even if the coins you collect are only worth the value stamped on them, they will be interesting. And, if you take care of them, who knows? They may become very valuable some day!

After you have learned a little about coins, try a few brain-teasers on your friends.

1. Name the one thing found on every United States coin.

2. Name three of the Presidents who are on United States coins.

3. What animal is printed on a United States nickel? (Here's where Linus gave up!)

4. What United States coin has George Washington on it?

5. Name two United States coins that have Indians on them.

The answers are on page 80.

Try making up some brain-teasers yourself. The more you know about coins, the harder your questions will be.

Linus is clever at doing magic tricks with his coins. Here's one of his favorites. (Don't let anyone see you do the first 8 steps.)

1. Cut a sheet of colored construction paper in half.

2. Put a transparent drinking glass down on one half of the paper. Trace around the rim of the glass with a pencil to make a circle.

3. Cut out the circle you drew, and erase any pencil marks that show.

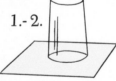

4. Put small dabs of glue on the rim of the glass.

5. Put the circle on the mouth of the glass and press firmly. Let the glue dry.

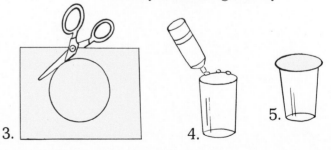

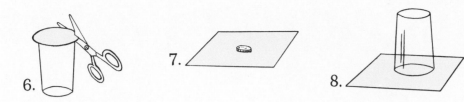

6. Trim off any paper that overlaps the rim.

7. Place a thin coin on the other half of the construction paper. (A dime is best.)

8. Put the glass down on the coin so that the colored circle covers it.

Now you are ready for your audience.

A. Tell the audience to look through the glass. Ask if they can see anything on the paper. Of course they won't see a thing!
B. Tell your audience that you will make a coin appear on the paper.
C. Cover the glass with a handkerchief.
D. Say "Abracadabra!"
E. Pick up the glass. Be sure you keep the handkerchief over the glass!

It's magic! A coin has appeared! If you like, you can now make the coin disappear. Just put the glass, still covered with the handkerchief, back over the coin, say your magic words, and then remove the handkerchief. Presto! The coin mysteriously disappeared. You can make the coin appear and disappear as many times as you wish.

Sally practiced and played this trick on Charlie Brown. He let her use some coins from his collection—and now he says they've disappeared!

Collecting Leaves

I'M SORT OF A FANATIC ABOUT SAVING THINGS...

YOU'VE NEVER SEEN MY LEAF COLLECTION, HAVE YOU, CHARLIE BROWN?

I HAVE A BLACK WILLOW, A BUR OAK, A SHAGBARK HICKORY, A GINKGO, A QUAKING ASPEN AND A WHITE ASH...

GANGWAY!!

YAHOO!!

..MY LEAF COLLECTION!

SCHULZ

There are more than a thousand different kinds of trees in the United States. So there will be many different leaves for you to collect no matter where you live—unless you live in the middle of the desert or in Copperhill, Tennessee. Many years ago, poison fumes from the copper refining industry in that town killed all the plants and trees. Now there aren't even any birds in the area.

BRING BACK BIRDS

LEAF POWER

Woodstock may not like it, but you really won't hurt a tree by picking a few leaves. The ideal way to collect leaves is to pick two from each kind of tree. Then when you display them you can show both sides of each kind of leaf. Your collection will be even more interesting if you collect leaves from the same kind of tree at different seasons. That way you can show the growth and change in color as the year progresses.

Start your collection with leaves from trees that grow in your own state or town or even just on your own block. Lucy was surprised to discover how many different kinds of trees grew right in her own backyard. As your collection begins to grow and you learn more about leaves, you will probably want to add specimens from much farther away.

When you go hunting for leaves, take a magazine with you and put the leaves between the pages to keep them from curling up. When you get home you can "press" the leaves. If you're a flower collector, you already know how to do that.

Charlie Brown didn't read the instructions and now he needs a new red maple leaf.

1. Lay each leaf on a piece of paper towel or newspaper. Make sure the stem is straight and the leaf tips lie flat.

2. Put another piece of paper over each leaf.

3. Stack up all your leaf "sandwiches" with extra newspaper in between.

4. Put some heavy books on top of the stack.

Your leaves will dry in about a week. Handle them very carefully, as they will be brittle.

If you have extra pressed leaves, you can make attractive designs to hang on your wall. Just glue the leaves to a piece of colored paper or fabric. Follow the instructions for making a collage on page 70.

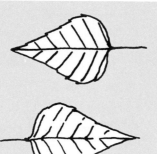

When your leaves are pressed, you can mount them on sheets of colored construction paper.

1. Put each kind of leaf on a separate sheet. If you are showing two samples of each leaf, be sure one faces up and one faces down.
2. Tape the leaves in place, or glue them with little dabs of rubber cement. (Good old Charlie Brown forgot to read the instructions again!)
3. On each sheet, write the name of the leaf and where and when you found it.

AMERICAN ELM-
LONG ISLAND, MAY 2

The leaf of each kind of tree has its own special shape, size, and color. Even the pattern of the veins is different in each kind of leaf. Trees that shed their leaves every fall have two types of leaves—simple and compound. A compound leaf has several leaflets on one stem.

A simple leaf is one single shape. Lucy refuses to put one in her collection. She likes things to be more complicated.

Look at each leaf you find and compare it with pictures in a guide book. You can borrow one from the library or buy your own. You'll discover that each tree has a common name and a Latin name.

Here are some of the leaves in Schroeder's collection. Maybe you'll find some of these on your block.

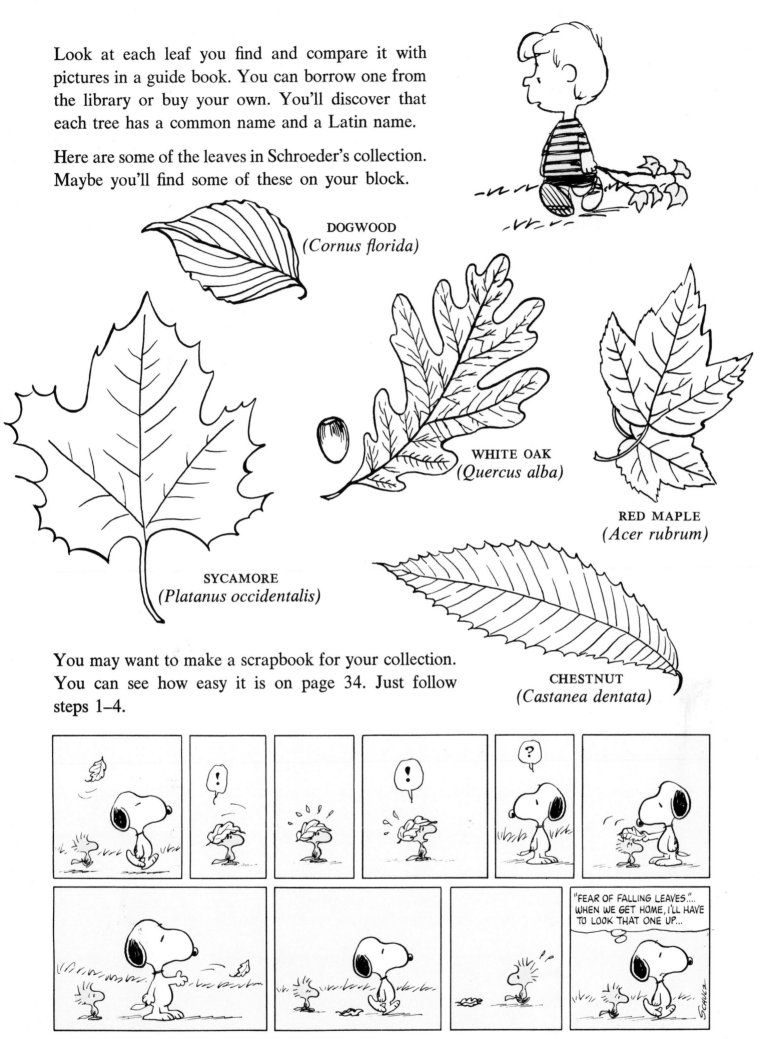

DOGWOOD
(Cornus florida)

WHITE OAK
(Quercus alba)

RED MAPLE
(Acer rubrum)

SYCAMORE
(Platanus occidentalis)

CHESTNUT
(Castanea dentata)

You may want to make a scrapbook for your collection. You can see how easy it is on page 34. Just follow steps 1–4.

"FEAR OF FALLING LEAVES."....
WHEN WE GET HOME, I'LL HAVE
TO LOOK THAT ONE UP...

When Lucy isn't jumping into leaves, she makes silhouette prints with them.

You can also make silhouette prints by using a toothbrush.

Cover your worktable with newspapers, as this can be messy—especially when Charlie Brown tries it.

1. Put a piece of colored construction paper on top of a piece of cardboard.
2. Pin a leaf on the paper by sticking straight pins through it into the cardboard.
3. Lightly spray the entire sheet of paper (the leaf, too) with a can of spray paint.
4. Let the paint dry before removing the pins and the leaf.

Now you have a spray print!

1. Pin a leaf to paper and cardboard, as you did for the spray print.
2. Dip an old toothbrush into a jar of tempera paint and hold it over the leaf.
3. Firmly slide a pencil along the bristles of the brush. Be sure you start at the far end of the brush and move the pencil toward you, or you'll spatter paint on yourself instead of the paper! Stop when the paper is covered with dots of paint.
4. Let the paint dry. Then take out the pins and lift off the leaf.

A silhouette spatter print!

Try experimenting with different colored paper and paints. You can make your own greeting cards with silhouette leaf prints. Holly leaves are perfect for Christmas cards.

As for Woodstock, big leaves make him nervous — he's collecting pine needles!

60

Collecting Fingerprints

You don't have to be a detective to collect fingerprints!

Collecting fingerprints is a unique hobby and with a little practice you can become an expert at it.

The fascinating thing about fingerprints is that no two are ever the same. That's why they are often used to identify people.

Look closely at your fingertip and you can see the lines that make up a fingerprint. There are three main fingerprint patterns:

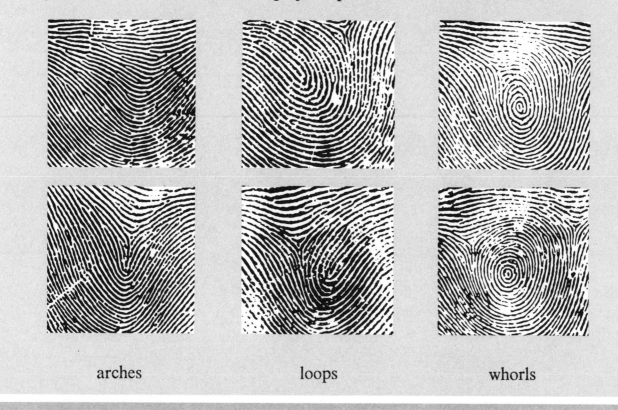

arches   loops   whorls

A fingerprint collection has to be kept in an orderly fashion. So before you start collecting, prepare a file box and some identification cards on which to keep each person's fingerprints. You will find instructions for making a file box on page 67. (Write letters of the alphabet on the divider cards.)

Here's how to make your identification cards:

1. Buy some index cards, or cut your own cards from lightweight cardboard.

2. Draw lines at the top for the name of the person whose fingerprints will be on the card and the date of fingerprinting.

3. In the middle, draw ten squares so you'll have a space for each fingerprint. Label the squares as shown on the card below. (Of course, you don't have to take a print of every finger. Even one is good identification.)

4. Draw a line at the bottom for the signature of the person you are fingerprinting.

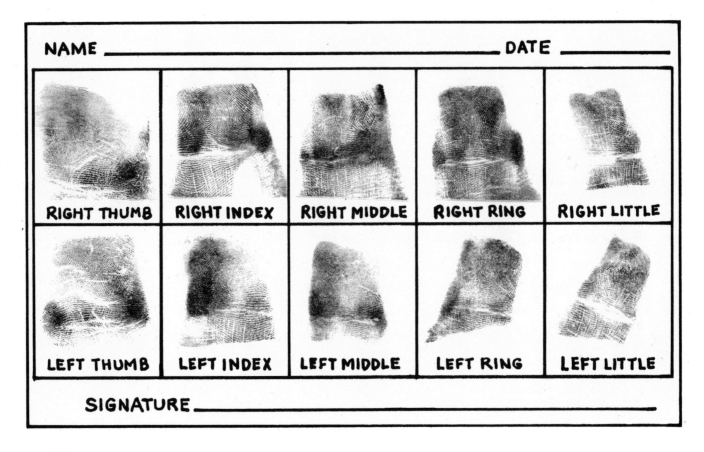

Now you are ready to finger-print. Taking fingerprints is fun, but you'll have to find a friend who is more cooperative than Charlie Brown!

Fingerprinting takes a little practice. After you've tried it a few times, you'll know how much ink to put on the finger and how much pressure is needed to get a clear print.

You can use an ordinary ink pad. Or you can buy printer's ink, a roller, and a flat glass tray in a hobby shop. Just roll a small amount of printer's ink thinly and evenly on the glass.

1. Tell your friend to relax!

2. Press your friend's finger on the ink pad. Or, if you're using printer's ink, carefully roll the finger over the inked glass. Then check that the finger is evenly inked, from the very tip to below the first joint.

3. Carefully roll the finger over the correct square on the identification card. Don't just press the finger down flat, or you'll get a smudged, incomplete print.

4. That's it! You have a fingerprint! Now you can fill up the card with the rest of your friend's prints.

5. Don't forget to ask for your friend's signature at the bottom of the identification card.

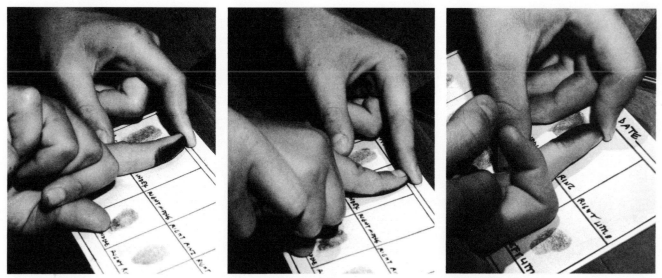

Instead of taking fingerprints directly from friends, you can search for hidden ones!

You can find them anywhere. People leave their fingerprints on everything they touch. Often you can't see the prints, but they're there! These "invisible" prints are called latent prints.

Sometimes you can see them by using a flashlight and a magnifying glass. But the best way to find latent fingerprints is to "dust" for them. After you find them, you can actually lift them up and transfer them to a card.

To do this you will need a small can of talcum powder, a roll of clear cellophane tape, and a small artist's brush.

Since it's easier to take fingerprints from smooth, hard surfaces, find a table or a glass that you think someone has touched recently.

If you are looking for prints on a dark surface, use white talcum powder right out of the can. If you are looking for them on a light-colored surface, you'll need black powder. Make your own by scraping a stick of charcoal with the edge of a knife blade. (You can buy charcoal in an art supply store.)

Here's how to dust for latent prints:

2.

1. Dip the brush lightly into the dusting powder. Tap off any extra powder. You only need a little bit. Watch out for dust storms!

2. With the brush, lightly dust the area where you think prints may have been left. The powder will stick to any prints. Do you see one?

3. When you find a clear print, tear off a piece of cellophane tape long enough to cover it. Carefully put the tape down over the dusted print. Then press evenly and gently on the tape. Be sure not to move it around.

3.

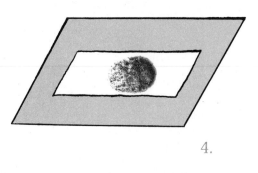
4.

4. Lift the tape up and stick it onto a small piece of paper. (If you're using white powder, put the tape on dark paper. If you're using black powder, you'll need light-colored paper.) If the print isn't clear, you may have used too much powder. Without dusting again, try another piece of tape on the same print.

5. Paste the paper with the latent fingerprint onto a card that can go into your file box.

6. See if you can discover whose print you've found by comparing it with the ones in your file. If you can, write the person's name on the card.

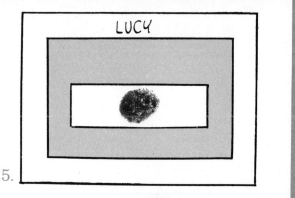
5.

LUCY

Remember! People leave fingerprints on any object they touch. So you can get any prints you want by handing someone a clean glass.

Here's a way to have extra fun with fingerprints. Put one or more on a piece of paper and see what kind of picture you can think up.

BY LINUS

BY LUCY

BY SCHROEDER

BY WOODSTOCK

BY CHARLIE BROWN

BY SALLY

BY SNOOPY

Collecting Postcards

When people go on a trip, they often send picture postcards to their friends. How many cards have you received? If you start a postcard collection, just think of all the different places you can see without even leaving home! You can pretend you are anywhere in the world you want to be. Snoopy got a postcard from one of his favorite stars and look what it's done to him!

Ask your family, friends, and neighbors if you can have any postcards they get. Also ask them to send cards to you when they go away. Even a little trip to a nearby town can rate a postcard! Charlie Brown hardly ever gets any mail, but he can buy postcards at drugstores, bookshops, card shops, post offices, and museums. That's a good way for anyone to begin a collection — or add to an established one. Postcards don't cost much.

Sally's collection got so large and varied that she decided to make a file for it. Here's how to make one for your collection:

1. Find a shoe box large enough to hold your postcards in an upright position.
2. Cut divider cards out of heavy paper. They should be almost as wide as the shoe box and taller than your postcards. Use them to divide your collection into the different subjects you are collecting.
3. Write the name of each subject at the top of a divider so you can see it when the card is in the box.

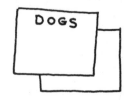

Once your collection is large, you can trade postcards with friends.

It's fun to collect cards that have pictures of your favorite things.

Peppermint Patty likes dogs so much, she's managed to collect 27 postcards of them. What's your favorite animal?

Collect cards of your favorite person. You can imagine who's on Schroeder's postcards!

Woodstock collects postcards of football players, and football stadiums, and footballs. Any sport is a great subject for a postcard collection.

Not everyone likes winter, but it's Lucy's favorite time of year. She collects postcards of winter scenes from all over the world.

Linus collects postcards with pictures of blankets. Maybe your favorite thing is easier to find on cards than his!

Snoopy would rather eat than do anything else. He collects postcards of food — particularly the kinds no one serves him!

Your favorite things might not be blankets or food. But whatever they are — start collecting.

You can hang up your postcards in your room if you like. Here is one way to do this:

1. Carefully cut slits in the top and bottom of each card you want to hang.
2. Thread a length of ribbon (or a piece of yarn) through the slits. Make sure the picture side of the card isn't covered.
3. Put as many cards as you wish on the ribbon. Leave enough ribbon at the bottom of the lowest card so it won't slip off.
4. Tie the ribbon to a bedpost or a lamp, or pin it to the wall.

If you want to see the messages on the back of your cards as well as the pictures on the front, make a mobile.

1. Thread a needle with a long piece of strong thread and tie a knot in one end.
2. Push the needle into the picture side of a card at center bottom and pull the thread through.
3. Bring the needle back up through the top center of the picture.
4. Put as many cards on the thread as you wish. Then push the needle up once through a large postcard (at side center), remove the needle, and tie a knot in the thread. Be sure the large postcard is at least twice the size of all the others you have used. (If you haven't got a large postcard, use a piece of colored cardboard, or simply tie the end of the thread to a wire hanger.)
5. Make several more strings with cards on them. Hang them all from the large card as in step 4.
6. Finally, push another threaded needle up through the center of the large card. This thread has to hold up the whole mobile, so make sure there's a sturdy knot at the end of it.
7. Hang your mobile near a window so that a breeze can turn all the cards around for you to see.

You can make a collage with your postcards. A collage is a work of art created by pasting different things onto a piece of paper or board. You can use the colors and shapes on your postcards to create a design. All you have to do is move the cards around — you can cut them up if you want — until you get an effect you like. Your design doesn't have to look like anything special — it just has to please you. Linus is very pleased with his collage!

A collage can be made up of a lot of different things, not just postcards. So paste down whatever else you think looks good — pieces of yarn, labels from bottles, buttons — anything!

To Charlie Brown

Here's something else you can do with your postcards. Make a treasure chest! Schroeder keeps marbles in his. What will you put in yours?

1. Choose ten postcards all the same size (or trim cards to the same size). Cut a square from each postcard. Each side should be as long as the postcard's shortest side. Then cut four large triangles from four of the squares.

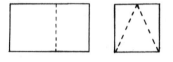

2. Thread a large-eyed needle with yarn, and tie a knot in one end of the yarn. Put two squares together, picture side to picture side. Sew them together with the yarn along one side, using a hemming stitch. Tie a knot in the yarn at the end of your last stitch so the yarn won't pull out of the cards. Then cut off the extra yarn.

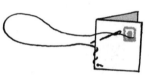

3. Open up the two squares. Place a third square, picture to picture, on one of the first two squares, and stitch them together. Then sew on a fourth square. Make sure the pictures on the squares all end up on the same side.

4. Fold your chain of squares in half, along the center line of stitching. The picture side of the cards should now be facing out. Sew the last two open sides of the squares together.

5. Pull the four squares open to form a box. Make a bottom for it by sewing on a fifth square. Its picture side should face up into the box. Then hem stitch along the top rim of the box. (This stitching is just for decoration.)

6. Sew the four triangles together to form a pyramid. Bend the cards into position as you sew. Be sure the pictures face out.

7. Make a bottom for the pyramid by sewing on the sixth square. Its picture side should face out.

8. Sew one bottom edge of the pyramid to the top of the box. Now your box has a lid.

9. If you want, add a button to the box and a loop of yarn to the lid to hold your treasure chest closed.

Now you won't have to bury your treasure anymore — unlike Snoopy!

If you have special postcards that you want to keep forever, make a scrapbook for them.

1. Use sheets of colored construction paper for the pages in the scrapbook—as many as you want. Use two more sheets (or two pieces of colored cardboard) for the front and back covers.

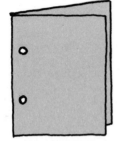

2. With a hole puncher or a pencil, punch two holes along the left side of each page and the covers. Make sure the holes are in the same place on every sheet!

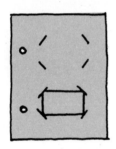

3. Carefully cut slits in the pages so that you can slide in the four corners of each postcard. Now you can take out the cards whenever you wish. If you are sure you won't want to remove them, just paste them on the pages.

4. Line up all the pages inside the covers. (Be sure to include some blank pages at the back.) Thread a piece of colored yarn through each set of holes, and tie the loose ends in a bow.

POSTCARDS
(SPECIAL ONES)

5. Write the title of your scrapbook on the front cover.

6. If you ever run out of pages in your scrapbook, just untie the yarn and add more sheets of paper to the back.

Who do you know that's going away soon and can send you lots of postcards? Poor Charlie Brown is still waiting for a postcard so he can start his collection.

Collecting Hats

Save your old hats and ask your family and friends for theirs. Look for hats in thrift shops and flea markets. Then try making some! With three basic shapes, you can create dozens of different hats. Just add paint, scraps of cloth, paper cutouts, or yarn to make the kind of hat you want.

TRIANGLE HAT

1. Get a piece of paper about 20 inches by 16 inches. Fold it in half, short end to short end.
2. Fold the top right corner over to the center.
3. Fold the top left corner over to the center.
4. Fold up the upper sheet remaining at the bottom.
5. Turn the hat over. Fold up the bottom to match the other side. The triangle hat makes a great birthday party hat. Just punch a hole in the center of each bottom fold and thread an 18-inch length of string through each hole. Tape each string in place. Now you can tie the hat under your chin.

BOWL HAT

1. This can get messy, so lay out some newspapers on your worktable and wear a smock.
2. Find a bowl big enough to fit on your head. Turn it upside down on the newspapers.
3. Cut up some sheets of newspaper into strips about six inches long and one inch wide.
4. In another bowl, mix one cup of flour and one cup of water into a smooth paste.
5. Lightly dip each strip of newspaper into the flour-and-water paste and lay it on the upside-down bowl. The strips should crisscross each other. Cover the entire bowl with four or five layers of strips.
6. Let the strips dry completely. This may take a day.
7. Carefully lift the hardened strips in one piece from the bowl. You may have to slip a knife edge under the hat to loosen it.
8. With scissors, cut around the edge of the hat to make it even. Now add your paint, feathers, lettering, or whatever you want!

TUBE HAT

1. Get a sheet of construction paper about 12 inches by 24 inches. Roll it into a tube.
2. Adjust the size of the tube so that it fits on your head. Then tape down the over-lapping end of paper.
3. Center the tube on top of another sheet of construction paper at least 12 inches by 12 inches. With a pencil, trace the outline of the tube on the flat paper.
4. Cut out the circle you just drew. Then cut another circle around the first one by trimming off the four corners of the sheet.
5. Cut slits about an inch long all the way around one end of the tube.
6. Slip the tube into the circle. Fold up the tabs at the slit end of the tube and tape them in place on the circle.

Put on a hat,
use your imagination, and you can be anyone at all.
Or, wear your favorite old hat and...

Here are some ways to learn more about your hobby.

1. Join a hobby club. Look in the classified "yellow pages" of your telephone directory for one near you.
2. Also check the "yellow pages" for stores that sell whatever you are collecting.
3. Write to the Superintendent of Documents, U.S. Government Printing Office, Washington, D.C. 20025. Ask to be put on their mailing list. They print many inexpensive pamphlets on hobbies.
4. Go to your school or public library. Ask the librarian to help you find books about your hobby. Some suggestions are listed below.
5. Subscribe to a magazine for people who have your hobby.

Suggested Books

General

World Book Encyclopedia. 1975. Chicago: Field Enterprises Educational Corporation. An encyclopedia that can tell you about almost anything.

Salny, Roslyn W. 1965. *Hobby Collections A-Z*. New York: Thomas Y. Crowell Company.

Bottles and Bottle Caps

Austen, Ferol. 1971. *Poor Man's Guide to Bottle Collecting*. Garden City, N.Y.: Doubleday & Company, Inc.

Sattler, Helen Roney. 1974. *Jar and Bottle Craft*. New York: Lothrop, Lee & Shepherd Co.

Buttons

Epstein, Diana. 1968. *Buttons*. New York: Walker & Co.

Coins

Hobson, Burton. 1970. *Coins You Can Collect*. New York: Hawthorn Books, Inc.

Reinfeld, Fred. 1971. *Coin Collectors' Handbook*. Garden City, N.Y.: Doubleday & Company, Inc.

Dolls and Puppets

Boylan, Eleanor. 1970. *How To Be A Puppeteer*. New York: E. P. Dutton & Co., Inc.

Heady, Eleanor F. 1974. *Make Your Own Dolls*. New York: Lothrop, Lee & Shepherd Co.

Lewis, Shari. 1967. *Making Easy Puppets*. New York: E. P. Dutton & Co., Inc.

Young, Helen. 1964. *Here Is Your Hobby: Doll Collecting*. New York: G. P. Putnam's Sons.

Fingerprints

Millimaki, Robert H. 1973. *Fingerprint Detective*. Philadelphia: J. B. Lippincott Company.

Flowers

Cutler, Katherine N. 1969. *From Petals to Pinecones: A Nature Art and Craft Book*. New York: Lothrop, Lee & Shephard Co.

Lobley, Priscilla. 1971. *Flower Making for Beginners*. New York: Taplinger Publishing Co.

Zim, Herbert S. and Alexander, Martin. 1950. *Flowers* (A Golden Nature Guide). New York: Western Publishing.

Hats

Wilcox, R. Turner. 1945. *The Mode In Hats and Headdress*. New York: Charles Scribner's Sons.

Leaves

Beetschen, Louis, editor. 1971. *Country Treasures*. New York: Pantheon/Knopf.

Foster, Laura Louise. 1970. *Keeping The Plants You Pick*. New York: Thomas Y. Crowell Company. Tells how to pick, preserve and mount plants.

Zim, Herbert S. and Alexander, Martin C. 1952. *Trees* (A Golden Nature Guide). New York: Western Publishing.

Maps

Epstein, Sam and Beryl. 1959. *The First Book of Maps and Globes*. New York: Franklin Watts, Inc.

The Grosset World Atlas. 1973. New York: Grosset & Dunlap.

Schere, Monroe. 1969. *The Story of Maps*. Englewood Cliffs, N.J.: Prentice-Hall, Inc.

The U.S. government prints maps of all the states, maps of other countries, nautical and aeronautical charts, and moon maps. If you want to know where to get any of these maps, write to Map Information Office, U.S. Geological Survey, Washington, D.C. 20025.

Menus and Place Mats

Many words on menus are French or Italian. Check in any standard dictionary under "Foreign Words and Phrases" for their meanings.

Waldo, Myra. 1962. *Dining Out in Any Language: The Menu Translator*. New York: Crown Publishers, Inc., Bantam Books. A dictionary of foreign menu words.

Postcards

Ask in your library for the following magazine article: *Fortune*. Chicago: Time, Inc., January, 1962, p. 101. "When Downtown Was a Beautiful Mess."

Rocks, Minerals and Fossils

Hyler, Nelson W. 1969. *The How and Why Wonder Book of Rocks and Minerals*. New York: Grosset & Dunlap.

Rhodes, Frank H., et al. 1962. *Fossils* (A Golden Nature Guide). New York: Western Publishing.

White, Anne Terry. 1959. *Rocks All Around Us*. New York: Random House.

Zim, Herbert S. and Shaffer, Paul R. 1957. *Rocks and Minerals* (A Golden Nature Guide). New York: Western Publishing.

Your local museum may have more information for you. It may also have a collection you may want to see.

Shells

Abbot, R. Tucker. 1969. *Seashells of North America* (A Golden Field Guide). New York: Western Publishing.

Beetschen, Louis, editor. 1971. *You Can Make Seaside Treasures*. New York: Pantheon/Knopf.

Low, Donald F. 1961. *The How and Why Wonder Book of Sea Shells*. New York: Grosset & Dunlap.

Stamps

Reinfeld, Fred. 1957. *Fun With Stamp Collecting*. Garden City, N.Y.: Doubleday & Company, Inc.

Turner, Jim. 1963. *Stamps: A Guide To Your Collection*. New York: J. B. Lippincott Company.

Villiard, Paul. 1974. *Collecting Stamps*. Garden City, N.Y.: Doubleday & Company, Inc.

Here's what the Peanuts gang ordered at the International Restaurant (page 49). Lucy: vegetable soup. Linus: pickled herring. Franklin: a tomato. Peppermint Patty: potato pancakes. Schroeder: roast beef. Charlie Brown: bread and water. Sally: chocolate ice cream. Snoopy: watermelon.

Answers to the coin brain-teasers on page 54.
1. The date. 2. Presidents Washington, Jefferson, Lincoln, Franklin D. Roosevelt, and Kennedy are all on United States coins. 3. A buffalo. 4. The Washington quarter. 5. The Indian-head cent and buffalo nickel.